Shailene Woodley

By Rebecca Sjonger

Crabtree Publishing Company
www.crabtreebooks.com

Crabtree Publishing Company

www.crabtreebooks.com

Author: Rebecca Sjonger
Publishing plan research and development: Reagan Miller
Photo research: Tammy McGarr
Editor: Kathy Middleton
Proofreader and Indexer: Wendy Scavuzzo
Designer: Ken Wright
Production coordinator and prepress technician: Ken Wright
Print coordinator: Margaret Amy Salter

Photographs:
Creative Commons: Mingle Media TV: title page
Everett Collection: © A24/Courtesy: p. 19 (top right);
Shutterstock: © s_bukley (cover); © Helga Esteb: pg 16, 19, 23
Getty Images: Amanda Edwards/WireImage: p. 4; Randy Holmes/© ABC via Getty Images: p. 6; Alo Ceballos/GC Images: p. 7; Jason Kempin: p. 8; Jason Merritt/FilmMagic: p. 10; Patricia Schlein/Star Max/GC Images: p. 15; Raymond Hall/GC Images: p. 20; Kevin Mazur/WireImage: p. 25; Lloyd Bishop/© NBC/NBCU Photo Bank via Getty Images: p. 26; eff Neira/© ABC via Getty Images: p. 27; Andrew H. Walker/WireImage: p. 28
Photofest: © Buena Vista: p. 11; © Twentieth Century Fox Film Corporation: pg 24
Keystone: © CARV/AKM-GSI: p. 17; ZUMAPRESS: p. 21
Photoshot: © Starstock: p. 5; © Photoshot/Collection Christophel: pp. 12, 13; © Starstock/Photoshot: pp. 14, 22
Seth Poppel/Yearbook Library: p. 9
Thinkstock: Alberto E. Rodriguez/Getty Images: p. 18

Library and Archives Canada Cataloguing in Publication

Sjonger, Rebecca, author
Shailene Woodley / Rebecca Sjonger.

(Superstars!)
Includes index.
Issued in print and electronic formats.
ISBN 978-0-7787-8081-6 (bound).--ISBN 978-0-7787-8085-4 (pbk.).--ISBN 978-1-4271-9987-4 (pdf).--ISBN 978-1-4271-9983-6 (html)

1. Woodley, Shailene--Juvenile literature. 2. Motion picture actors and actresses--United States--Biography--Juvenile literature. 3. Television actors and actresses--United States--Biography--Juvenile literature. I. Title. II. Series: Superstars! (St. Catharines, Ont.)

PN2287.W645S56 2015 j791.4302'8092 C2014-907841-2
C2014-907842-0

Library of Congress Cataloging-in-Publication Data

Sjonger, Rebecca.
Shailene Woodley / Rebecca Sjonger.
pages cm. -- (Superstars!)
Includes index.
ISBN 978-0-7787-8081-6 (reinforced library binding) -- ISBN 978-0-7787-8085-4 (pbk.) -- ISBN 978-1-4271-9987-4 (electronic pdf) -- ISBN 978-1-4271-9983-6 (electronic html)
1. Woodley, Shailene--Juvenile literature. 2. Actors--United States--Biography--Juvenile literature. I. Title.

PN2287.W645S56 2015
791.4302'8092--dc23
[B]

2014045072

Crabtree Publishing Company

Printed in Canada/042015/BF20150203

www.crabtreebooks.com 1-800-387-7650

In Canada: We acknowledge the financial supportof the Government of Canada through the Canada Book Fund for our publishing activities.

Published in Canada
Crabtree Publishing
616 Welland Ave.
St. Catharines, ON
L2M 5V6

Published in the United States
Crabtree Publishing
PMB 59051
350 Fifth Avenue, 59th Floor
New York, New York 10118

Published in the United Kingdom
Crabtree Publishing
Maritime House
Basin Road North, Hove
BN41 1WR

Published in Australia
Crabtree Publishing
3 Charles Street
Coburg North
VIC 3058

CONTENTS

Words that are defined in the glossary are in bold type the first time they appear in the text.

Hey Shai!

The year 2014 was a star-maker for young actress Shailene Woodley. Her roles in the movies *Divergent* and *The Fault in Our Stars* brought her international attention. But Shailene was not an overnight success. She worked hard to reach the level she is at today.

Rise to Fame

Shailene first became known to millions of teenagers as Amy Juergens in the teen TV drama *The Secret Life of the American Teenager*. After five successful seasons, Shailene decided to focus on acting in movies. Her first major film role playing George Clooney's daughter in *The Descendants* proved to be her **breakout** performance. Once she got her foot in the door to Hollywood, she kicked it wide open—in her quiet, zen sort of way. A series of other incredibly successful movies including *The Spectacular Now*, *Divergent*, and *The Fault in Our Stars* quickly followed, catapulting Shailene to stardom.

Young Shailene joined an all-star cast, which included George Clooney, in her first big movie role.

He Said It

"Shailene can do whatever she wants. If she wants to be a movie star, she has it. If she wants to change the world, she will. Her talent and kindness go hand in hand."
—George Clooney, interview in *Vanity Fair*, June 2014

In the Spotlight

As Shailene's fame grows, so does the media's attention on her. She is friendly and open during interviews. However, the outgoing actress would much rather chat about her projects and passions than her love life. She happily describes her **survivalist** training, for example. She is learning to live on the natural resources found in the wild. Shailene is also a **herbalist**. That means she uses many different herbs to help with healing.

Honk If You Love Shai!

Shailene's mom chose her first name before the star's parents even met! She saw "Shai" on a license plate and knew she wanted it to be part of her daughter's name someday. Family and friends call her Shai, which is pronounced "Shay."

Low-Key Style

Shailene dresses up for photo shoots and special events, but the actress is not very interested in fashion. She says her whole wardrobe fits in one suitcase and is mainly secondhand. She prefers her barefoot-style rubber sports shoes to high heels. Shailene rarely wears makeup—although she makes a great lip stain with cooked beets!

Shailene grew interested in protecting the environment as a teen. She has even stopped to pick up litter during interviews!

She Said It

"I do think it's fun sometimes to dress up for the Oscars or for certain events—I get to be like a five-year-old again, wearing my Cinderella dress. But for some events where it's a more casual vibe, I just want to be me."

—From interview by actress Emma Stone in *Interview Magazine*, September 2014

A Star Is Born

Shailene Diann Woodley was born in Simi Valley, California, on November 15, 1991. Her dad, Lonnie, was a principal when she was a child. Later, he switched to working as a family therapist. Her mom, Lori, is a school counselor. Shailene has one younger brother, named Tanner. Their parents divorced when Shailene was 14 years old, but the family remains close.

Shailene and her mom started a **charity** called All It Takes. It **promotes** anti-bullying, teamwork, and youth leadership.

She Said It

"Living from your deep heart and having compassion: It's what I think about every single day. It's one of the biggest lessons I've taken from childhood."
—Interview in *InStyle* magazine, June 2014

Spotted in Class

Shailene began taking acting classes at age five. She enjoyed them as a fun way to express herself. A **talent agent** spotted her during a class and got in touch with her parents. The Woodleys lived less than an hour away from Hollywood, but Shailene's mom did not know what an agent was. Luckily, she figured it out. Shailene appeared in her first commercial at age six.

Shailene's school yearbook photo

The Three Rules

Shailene's parents both supported her dream of being an actress, but only if she followed three rules. Shailene had to stay the same person she had always been, keep doing well in school, and have fun acting.

The Early Years

Young Shailene quickly landed parts in commercials. She was in so many that she lost count! In 1999, Shailene got a small part in her first television movie, *Replacing Dad*. She got many TV roles after that. Shailene also played a few **recurring** characters on TV series, such as *Crossing Jordan*. Her first starring role came in 2005's made-for-TV movie *Felicity: An American Girl Adventure*. Two years later, she got a small part in *Moola,* her first big-screen film.

Her best guess is that she was in close to 60 commercials by the time she turned 11!

School Spirit

Shailene went to public school in Simi Valley while acting on the side. Most of her friends and classmates did not make a big deal out of her being on TV. The bubbly actress was very social and involved in school activities, such as pep rallies and football games. Since acting was already such a big part of her life, Shailene did not join her high school's drama club. Instead, she sang in the school choir every year.

Staying Positive

Shailene also tried out for many roles that she did not get. The young actress really wanted a part in the movie *I Am Sam*. She was disappointed when Dakota Fanning got it instead. But Shailene's dad helped her to stay positive and support other girls in **auditions**.

Win Some, Lose Some

Shailene describes herself as a "late bloomer." After playing Kaitlin Cooper on six episodes of *The O.C.*, she lost the role when the show needed her to look older.

Shailene knew Josh Hutcherson (shown here in the movie *Bridge to Terabithia*) and *iCarly*'s Miranda Cosgrove from acting classes and auditions.

She Said It

"I loved that it was a challenge. I loved that I got told 'no' 500 times, because it was something I had to work hard at. It was never a competitive thing for me, and it still isn't."

—Interview in *Marie Claire* magazine, March 2014

Big Break

At age 15, Shailene landed the lead role in *The Secret Life of the American Teenager*. Her character, Amy Juergens, gets pregnant the summer before starting high school. The TV series follows Amy as she juggles being a mom, daughter, sister, student, friend, and girlfriend. Shailene describes the show as a **soap opera** for young people.

Secret Life was popular with viewers, but the show got mixed reviews from TV **critics**.

Hitting the Books

When Shailene got the part in *Secret Life*, she no longer had time to attend high school classes. Her principal arranged for a teacher to bring her schoolwork weekly. The hard-working actress brought it to the set with her. Shailene graduated and went to prom with her classmates.

Not-So-Secret Strife

At first, Shailene liked how *Secret Life* dealt with **controversial** topics such as teen pregnancy. However, she later felt Amy's actions were at odds with her own views. She also felt trapped by her **contract** with ABC Family. The network got to choose which acting projects Shailene could do on breaks from shooting the show. Aware that actors are not always regularly employed, the sensible star also spent part of one break working at an American Apparel store in New York City.

Body Issues

Shailene was a self-conscious teen. Not only did she feel she was too skinny, she also had to wear a plastic **brace** on her upper body to correct **scoliosis**, or a curved spine.

At the end of the first season of *Secret Life*, Shailene's character Amy Juergens gives birth to her son John.

She Said It

"I had to wear a brace for two years and I embraced the brace. I accepted it, and I lived with it. I found cute things to wear with baggy T-shirts. And it didn't affect the acting at all. I would take the brace off during filming and then put it back on during the breaks."
—From *The Orange County Register*, August 2013

Hitting the Big Screen

Shailene shot her first big film while on a break from *The Secret Life of the American Teenager*. She played Alexandra King in *The Descendants*. George Clooney starred as Alexandra's father. In the movie, the Kings struggle in their relationships with one another after Alexandra's mom ends up in a coma after a boating accident.

George and Shailene

Her Pal, George

Working with superstar George Clooney made Shailene nervous at first. She soon found out that he was welcoming and friendly with everyone on set. Now she describes him as like a big brother. For his part, Clooney told a reporter that he would be happy to adopt Shailene!

She Said It

"I was a successful child actor, but I wasn't a famous child actor…When The Descendants *came out, I felt pressure for the first time. I'd been acting since I was 5, but I'd never really done any photo shoots or interviews, and I certainly had never been asked over and over about my Oscar chances."*
—Interview in *New York Magazine*, June 2014

Hawaiian Life

The movie was filmed in Hawaii. Shailene arrived a month early to get used to the slower pace of life there. She loved the natural beauty of Hawaii and spent a lot of her time outdoors. Wearing the brace to straighten her spine for two years had left her out of shape. Shailene went on hikes and became stronger. She says her lifestyle changed forever during her four months filming on location in Hawaii.

Almost Quit!

The huge success of *The Descendants* placed a lot of pressure on Shailene. For a while, she thought about quitting show business. She loved acting, though. To move forward, she decided not to care what others thought of her or wanted her to do next.

Acting or Reacting?

Describing her style of acting in *The Descendants*, Shailene said it felt as if she was not really acting. Instead, she just reacted to the story and other actors. Famed director Alexander Payne also helped guide her. In a **standout** scene, Shailene sobbed underwater after getting bad news about her mother. She called it a therapy session in which she could let out all her emotions. Critics were impressed with her performance.

The Trouble With TV

Shailene had her choice of projects after *The Descendants*. But the rising star could not just do whatever she wanted. She had two years left on her contract with *Secret Life*. She had to fit in other work around her TV show.

Popular media often tries to link Shailene romantically with actors she works with, like Daren Kagasoff from *Secret Life*.

Hollywood Rumble

In 2011, Shailene appeared as a gang member in the music video for "Our Deal" by the band Best Coast. The 10-minute-long video tells the love story of teens from rival gangs, the Day Trotters and Night Creepers. Many young stars, including Chloë Grace Moretz and Tyler Posey, are in the video. Actress Drew Barrymore directed it. Shailene loved the positive vibe that Barrymore created on the set.

Superhero to Zero

In 2013, Shailene got a small part in her first big-budget action movie, *The Amazing Spider-Man 2*. Shailene learned how to ride a motorcycle and dyed her hair red for her scenes which introduced her character Mary Jane Watson. In the end, the director decided to cut the character from the film because she took focus away from Spiderman's love story with Gwen Stacy played by Emma Stone. At first, Shailene was upset and wondered whether she had done a bad job. As usual, however, the upbeat actress respected the decision and moved forward.

Shailene filmed four scenes playing the role of Mary Jane, made famous in the previous Spider-Man film series by Kirsten Dunst.

She Said It

"I don't want to play the game of cat and mouse, where I have to do this part so I can get that part. If it's meant to be it's meant to be."
—From *Los Angeles Times* website, November 2011

Spectacular Star

The final episode of *Secret Life* aired in June 2013. Just a few months later, Shailene was onscreen again. In *The Spectacular Now*, nerdy Aimee Finicky falls in love with party boy Sutter Keely. Rising star Miles Teller plays Sutter. Shailene says the story was like her own first romance, which was with a cooler boy. It must have ended well, because she remains in touch with her first boyfriend!

Both Shailene and co-star Miles Teller won a Special Jury Award for Acting at the Sundance Film Festival.

She Said It

"I'm very, very proud of it. I think it's really exciting and different and beautiful. There aren't a lot of films about adolescents or quote-unquote coming-of-age films that are realistic nowadays. This is a really truthful birds'-eye look at what it's like to be in high school right now."—Interview about *The Spectacular Now* in *Indiewire*, January 2013

Natural Beauty

For most of the movie, Shailene did not wear makeup. She wanted Aimee to look like a real teen. The actress felt exposed at times when watching herself on the big screen. She was glad that she took the risk, though, because she felt it made the film better.

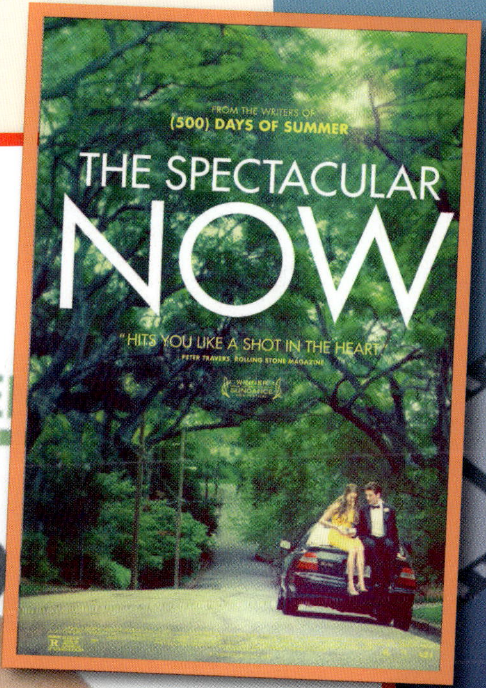

Books to Film

The plots of *The Descendants*, *The Spectacular Now*, and most of Shailene's later movies are based on popular novels. She read the books along with the scripts. Preparing this way gave her a better feel for the characters' whole histories.

A Huge Year

Shailene and Miles Teller met again onscreen in 2014. This time they played enemies in the hit movie *Divergent*. Shailene was the first choice to play the lead role of Beatrice "Tris" Prior. However, she almost turned down the part. Based on Veronica Roth's popular young adult **trilogy**, *Divergent* had a massive budget. Shailene was not sure how she felt about starring in such a huge movie. She also did not want to lock herself into a series after *The Secret Life of the American Teenager*. Finally, she did not want the level of attention the stars of *Twilight* and *The Hunger Games* had on them. Shailene asked for advice from someone who knew exactly how she felt—*The Hunger Games* star Jennifer Lawrence. Jennifer told Shailene the good things that would come from being in the movie would outweigh the bad.

The movie studio liked the fact that Shailene, like Tris, looked like an average girl.

Facing Her Fears

In the movie, Tris is expected to join her family's selfless **faction**, called Abnegation. She chooses instead to become part of the brave faction, called Dauntless. To become members of Dauntless, candidates must face whatever scares them the most in a test called a "fear landscape." People often ask Shailene what would be in her fear landscape. The actress describes being trapped in a deep-water submarine or in outer space. However, she also admits that she enjoys the rush of excitement that can come with fear.

In *Divergent*, Tris must pass a test by facing her deepest fears—and betrayal.

She Said It

*"I stole this answer from [*Divergent *author] Veronica Roth…I would choose to be factionless. I wouldn't want to be a part of any one faction and be living by a specific set of rules."*

—Interview in *The Daily Beast*, March 2014

Let's Get Physical

Playing Tris required Shailene to do much more physical work than she had done in other films. What characters say and do in action movies was also new to her. Shailene told the *Daily Express* that when she struggled, co-star Zoë Kravitz told her, "Sometimes it's fun to just do things that don't make sense in real life."

Shailene and Kate Winslet

Girl Power

Shailene values the way Tris interacts with her best friend Christina, played by Kravitz. She would like to see more strong female friendships onscreen. The actress formed an offscreen friendship with Kate Winslet, who plays villain Jeanine Matthews. Winslet is one of Shailene's acting **influences** because of her skills and enthusiasm on set.

Stay Tuned

Divergent hit theaters in March 2014. Shailene began shooting its **sequel**, *Insurgent*, just two months later for release in March 2015. *Allegiant*, the third book in the series, is going to be split into two movies. Fans will have to wait until 2017 for the entire story to appear on big screens.

Dating Co-Stars?

Many *Divergent* fans hoped Shailene and Theo James were dating, but they are not a real-life couple. Shailene says she is a big fan of **astrology**. She's a Scorpio and relies on star signs to test compatibility.

A Star in *Our Stars*

Shailene's second movie in 2014 gave her the chance to display a different type of bravery. In *The Fault in Our Stars,* she plays a teen dying from cancer. Based on the bestselling novel by John Green, the film tells the love story of Hazel and Augustus. Shailene had built up a lot of muscle for *Divergent*, and *The Fault in Our Stars* started shooting only a month later. She had to go from fit to very unhealthy-looking fast. To play Hazel, she gave up her favorite workouts, barefoot running, and yoga. Shailene looked so unwell that some people thought she was actually sick. It gave her a better understanding of how cancer patients are treated.

Fans of the book were excited about the movie. An online preview got over 20 million views!

She Said It

"[Short hair is] actually more maintenance than my long hair because when I wake up in the morning I look like a cockatoo, but as soon as I get in the shower, then it goes down."
—Interview in *USA Today*, March 2014

Hair for Hazel

Shailene knew she would have to cut her long hair to play Hazel. She had spent years growing her hair as long as possible. The actress saw it as a symbol of her strength. On the day of the big haircut, Shailene was extremely emotional, and shared photos of herself at the hairdresser during the cut. Then she urged fans to join her in donating their hair to the charity Children With Hair Loss. She called the hair **drive** "Hair for Hazel." Many donors posted online photos of themselves holding their hair donations.

Shailene now loves her shorter hair. In fact, she would go shorter—or even bald!

A Dark Turn

Shailene's third movie released in 2014 was very different from the first two. In *White Bird in a Blizzard*, she plays Kat Connors, a teen whose mother mysteriously disappears. Kat is left to deal with the loss alongside her dreary father. The actress describes it as darker than her previous work.

Just Say No to Selfies!

The number of Shailene's fans exploded in 2014. The star is kind when she meets fans. She does not feel the need to share details of her private life with them through social media, though. In fact, Shailene only carries a phone when she needs one for work. She deleted her Instagram account when she decided the photos focused too much on how she looked.

Up until 2013, Shailene used Twitter, but only to keep in touch with faraway friends. Her tweets are still online. They focus on her passions, not her fame.

Keeping It Real

Shailene greets each person she meets with a hug. Connecting with people is very important to her. On *The Tonight Show*, she told host Jimmy Fallon, *"I love hugging, right? It's like I'm real, you're real, let's hug it out."*

Judge Woodley

Shailene often says if she was not an actress, she would probably work with food. She enjoys each part of it, from planting and harvesting, to cooking and eating. The actress rarely watches TV. When she does, however, she enjoys reruns of the cooking show *Top Chef*. Its spinoff, *Top Chef Duels*, invited her to be a guest judge in August 2014. In Shailene's honor, the cooking focused on **foraging**, or finding wild foods. She shared some of her own foraging and cooking stories on the show.

Shailene cooking with Clinton Kelly, host of *The Chew*.

She Said It

"I've met people where I'm like, 'Hi, I'm Shai', and they can't even see me because they're screaming, and I'm making eye contact with them, but they're not there. And that, to me, is weird."

—From *Vanity Fair's Hollywood* website, June 2014

What's Next?

Shailene says she has no strategy for which movies she makes. She appears in a wide range of roles and tries not to be **typecast**, or play the same kind of character more than once. But she does feel at though she has outgrown young adult movie roles. Her dream job would be to play singer/songwriter Stevie Nicks in a film. She would also like to try her hand at comedy. Beyond acting, Shailene would like to attend college, travel the world, and practice herbalism.

She told *Women's Wear Daily* in May 2012, "I would love to act for the rest of my life, but I also know that it could be taken away in a day. It's something I've always loved, but it's nothing I've ever revolved my entire life around. I have many other passions as well."

Dream Team

Shailene hopes to work one day with actress Mélanie Laurent, actors Mark Ruffalo and Ewan McGregor, and director Cameron Crowe.

Timeline

1991: Shailene Diann Woodley is born on November 15 in Simi Valley, California

1996: Five-year-old Shailene is discovered by an agent at an acting lesson and soon begins appearing in commercials

1999: Her first role is "Little Girl" in the made-for-television movie *Replacing Dad*

2001–2007: She lands parts in many television shows, including *The District* and *The O.C.*, and television movies such as *Felicity: An American Girl Adventure*

2007: Shailene gets her first movie role in *Moola*

2008–2013: She appears in her first starring role as Amy Juergens on the television show *The Secret Life of the American Teenager*

2011: Her first big movie role in *The Descendants* is a huge critical success

2011: Along with several other young stars, she plays a gang member in the music video for Best Coast's "Our Deal"

2012: Shailene wins her first major award, Best Supporting Female for *The Descendants*, at the Independent Spirit Awards

2013: Her scenes as Mary Jane Watson are cut from The *Amazing Spider-Man 2*.

2013: The final episode of *The Secret Life of the American Teenager* airs in June

2013: *The Spectacular Now*, a teen romance starring Shailene and Miles Teller, is released

2014: Shailene plays Tris in the first of four planned *Divergent* movies

2014: She appears with Ansel Elgort in *The Fault in Our Stars*

2014: She stars in the adult thriller *White Bird in a Blizzard*

Glossary

astrology The practice of using the stars to predict the future
audition An interview for an acting role
brace A hard device that gives body support
breakout To suddenly become famous or noticed
charity An organization that helps people in need
contract A legal agreement
controversial Describing something that causes public conflict or disagreement
critic A person who reviews TV shows or movies
drive A campaign to reach a goal
faction A smaller group with the same views found within a large community
forage To search for food in the wild
herbalist Someone who uses plants for medical treatments
influence Something or someone that affects or shapes someone's life in an important way
promote To share information about a product or idea to encourage others to buy it or support it
recurring Occurring more than one time
scoliosis A medical condition in which a person's spine curves sideways
sequel A film whose story shows the events that happened after a previous film
soap opera A television show that follows the daily lives of a group of characters
standout Describes something that is exceptional
survivalist A person who has the skills needed to live outdoors without assistance
talent agent A person who books jobs for actors and other people in the entertainment industry
trilogy A series of three closely related books
typecast Repeatedly assigned to play the same type of role or character